T0198429

Surface Tension

POEMS BY ELAINE EQUI

COFFEE HOUSE PRESS :: MINNEAPOLIS :: 1989

Some of these poems have appeared in The Paris Review, Paper Air, Central Park, o.blék, Ploughshares, Gargoyle, New American Writing, North American Review, Aerial, St. Mark's Newsletter, The American Voice, LAICA Journal, Poetry Motel, Black and White, B City, Shiny International, Forehead, and The Brooklyn Review.

"Geisha" is reprinted by permission of The Quarterly.

Fifteen of the poems were also published as part of a chapbook, *Accessories*, by The Figures Press, 1988.

Cover art: "Empirical Moments" by Christian Haub, courtesy of the Anne Plumb Gallery.
Back cover photo by Becket Logan.

The publisher thanks the following organizations whose support helped make this book possible: The National Endowment for the Arts, a federal agency; The Jerome Foundation; and United Arts.

Coffee House Press books are distributed to trade by Consortium Book Sales and Distribution, 213 East Fourth Street, Saint Paul, Minnesota 55101. Our books are also available through all major library distributors and jobbers, and through most small press distributors, including Bookpeople, Bookslinger, Inland, Pacific Pipeline, and Small Press Distribution. For personal orders, catalogs or other information, write to: Coffee House Press
27 North Fourth Street, Suite 400, Minneapolis, Mn 55401.

Library of Congress Cataloging in Publication Data

Equi, Elaine.
    Surface Tension : poems / by Elaine Equi.
        p.   cm.
    ISBN 0-918273-54-4 : $8.95
    I. Title.
PS3555.Q5S8   1989
811'.54 — dc20   89-38597
                                        CIP

Contents

To My Parents

Tao

To go
round the world
with a flair
on a matchhead

from wharf
to ant farm

observing
all the signs
by rote

sad trot
charred nettles

the dog-eared webs
that hone the ether

until and then

furtive as a werewolf
you reappear
o path

Geisha

Intrigued
the room
entered itself
with the tiny steps
of a mermaid
with a mustache
of orange blossom
with an abyss
dangling from
one pierced ear.

What We Look Forward To

To open like
so many eyes
in the body

big and odd
as the moon
or speech
rushing up
a mountain

after a long illness
I said there is
this book
you would enjoy
and must really
read though it
isn't very good

there are lots
of windows in it
held together
by no more
than a thought

just as you
are no more
than a thought

that I think
while looking out
of those windows

which open like
so many eyes
in the body

for to enter
into its ledger
forces a change
in perspective
not only a new way
of seeing but
also of being

all that you know
and are
no more than
a thought

but one that
I think
nearly all
of the time.

Invoice

Deliver boat
with mirrored oar
off veneer avenue.

Inflate dog.

Assemble teacup labyrinth.

Glue chair to wall.
Extend wall to accomodate
upscale sweep of eye
following curve.

Place egg
under pendulum timer.

Goldleaf ice.

Stuff pillows
in aquariums.

Fill coffins
with sand.

When guests arrive
ignore them.

A Date with Robbe-Grillet

What I remember didn't happen.
Birds stuttering.
Torches huddled together.
The cafe empty, with no place to sit.

Birds stuttering.
On our ride in the country
the cafe empty, with no place to sit.
Your hair was like a doll's.

On our ride in the country
it was winter.
Your hair was like a doll's
and when we met it was as children.

It was winter
when it rained
and when we met it was as children.
You, for example, made a lovely girl.

When it rained
the sky turned the color of Pernod.
You, for example, made a lovely girl.
Birds strutted.

The sky turned the color of Pernod.
Within the forest
birds strutted
and we came upon a second forest

within the forest
identical to the first.
And we came upon a second forest
where I was alone

identical to the first
only smaller and without music
where I was alone
where I alone could tell the story.

My Illustrious Gargoyle Ancestors

Blame it on genetics.

How one held a book
above a bakery.

How one was known
as the architect of love.

How one pointed the way to a dry cleaners
during the Renaissance.

Their grimaces flickering
above my crib.

The wordless shape
of things to come.

When I bit a tourist.
When I strangled a ballerina.

When I shut myself up in the vault.
Blame it on genetics.

A span as a gadabout
and then it was back to the slab

like a stone thrown through the centuries
which briefly mistakes itself for a bird.

Folk Dance

1. Carrying a tray.
2. Using a camera.
3. An undetermined celebration.
4. Up and down the stairs like
   the chambermaid in *The Dead*
   who says "men are all palaver
   and such as they can get."
5. Asparagus peeking out from
   under the salmon.
6. Coolness outside. Sky by Turner.
7. A square scarf folded to make
   a triangle.

Maria Callas

Canaries faint
when caged
by the
metallic ardor
of your voice

filing its way
through the bars

as if
you intended
to pluck
the unfinished song

from their lungs
and devour it.

There is still
a touch of
the ancient myths

about you
though classically trained
as wild-eyed and tragic

to the opulence
of opera
you bring

a harsh
elemental reality

vinegar stored
in an oak casket

salt poured
on an enemy's wounds.

Crime and the Classics

That the wages of sin
are Dickens and Melville
is what I learned from TV
where the teacher says,
"Roberto, put the switchblade away
and read aloud for us."
And the warden says,
"These punks are not creative.
If they were, they would be robbing banks
instead of 7-11's.
What they need is good background."
So class is moved
to the prison library
where, while awaiting trial, our hero
reads all great books of the Western World
but gets the chair anyway.
It is later than the late show for him
dear reader,
but for you, the choice
between book or movie still remains.
Please, weigh it carefully.

Another Form of Suicidal Behavior

Even in this heat
they won't stop wearing all black

leather and mascara.
God it must be awful

like being a nun
in the old days.

I used to love watching nuns sweat
but these kids really suffer

and pay a high price for having watched
too many episodes of "The Munsters."

Some will certainly collapse
before they even reach

the Chinese restaurant
on the corner

and one has the distinct impression
that those who do survive

will never look
totally cool again.

Lesbian Corn

In summer
I strip away
your pale kimono.
Your tousled hair too,
comes off in my hands
leaving you
completely naked.
All ears and
tiny yellow teeth.

Approaching Orgasm

Under a green bough
                        history expires.
As into the well I dive
                        knowing well
that I shall return empty-handed
or clutching only the ragged outline
                        of you and you.
Dear me,
but in summer a great horniness
overwhelms us like a tidal wave
                        of sleep.
Outside and in, everything is blurred,
fuzzy, partially melted.
I am buying peaches
and I have a great desire
                        to eat one
flaunting its curve in the market.
Also today I went to the library
but it feels as though I am returning
from a much longer journey
                        perhaps
all the way back from the Nile.
Since my eyes are closed
much of the time, I can't be sure,
still it seems Cleopatra's voice
was calling me
                        as with a thud
workmen dropped the walls back in place.
Strange isn't it,
how views change
and now I approach orgasm
like one taking a day off.
It is simply blank space
                        on the calendar

but of course, in other cultures
it means something else
and must be approached
in an entirely different way.

Cages Sway

Skeletal prattle
in roomy

song
you are empty now

but cast your
barbaric shadow

everywhere at once
like flame licking

the wall between
this world and others.

Martha Graham

1.
In 1923
for the Greenwich
Village Follies

you performed
three dances
one Oriental
one Moorish

and one
with a large veil.

You said:
"Grace is your
relationship
to the world"

a deep-rooted
inclination
to converse

and just as poetry
is not about words
nor math about numbers

so too the dance
is not about its steps.

2.
With your spooky
Franz Kline makeup
and adolescence
of Indian maidens

the daughter
of Dr. George Graham
a specialist
in nervous disease

you dance
not with lyrical hands
but with
the nervous system

capricious and sterile
as a guillotine
for swans

dark fins
circling the white
of the eyeball.

Premonition

How is it
no one but me
sees you
behind the door
in ordinary rooms
not spirit
or flesh
but insect light
flickering.

Crusade

At some point
while still living
here
I had already
moved away
and begun
growing up
on nothing but

the novacaine
of pure adventure.

A spiky planet

where I knew
many fewer words

those small
wildflowers

        white and red

not even their names.

At the End of Summer

for Louis Zukofsky

Go on
Mr. Tree Fugue
I'm listening.

Waking to a Lullaby

                            the
earth breeds
tulip and onion bulbs
        asleep
in their lumpy crib.
Such sweetness
        in the air
is for them
not you
who tread day's nursery
sluggish
cultivating
ready again to lie down
        head heavy
over the plow,
the page.

At the Mall

They
do the gathering
for us
      take it all in
and give back
choices
      however limited.
They keep it together
      music   art
knows its place
in the system.
Money is refreshing
and the salespeople
      seem genuinely concerned
not so much
about music   art
or us
but about continuity
or maybe harmony
the shape
      that each transaction
takes in the larger context
of the day
as in
      "have a good one"
endlessly chanted mantra
to the patron saint of cash flow.

The Ezra Pound Cake

Composed in the "rag and bone shop
of the heart"
it rises, many-tiered,
to uphold the wisdom of old men
by its bony Grecian columns.
They are adorable
when festooned with rags
(the men) but weary
oh so weary of the world.
Weary also are the guests.
Dreary the day Odysseus returned.
Solemn the suitors
that were turned away empty-handed.

The Dairy Queen at Sunset

After each private episode
one re-enters society anew

amid cowlicks of light
a swirl of voices

sharp in the nose
as razorblades of grass

sharp is "the taste
of noise" after silence

the cool residue
of an electrical disturbance

carried home
in a paper cup.

Black Halo

Darkness the size of a plate.
Bottles squat like dwarves.
The forest turned on the Victrola.
The fierce calligraphy of her hair
began the story with these words:
"It was the perfect place but not time
or else it was the perfect time
but not place." A stray integer
miscalculated the distance. A robot
was seen carrying off a child.

Rural Geometry

You confuse me
as a cow's nipples
would confuse me

but the steady click
of give and take
draws the line.

A perimeter where
from your point
of you

pulse
divides the protocol
into a roll call

of fluent shapes
more than just
an expanse

of green things
you settle for me
like dew on fear.

Crickets Crush Woman

Can't shake
the "I'm next" feeling.

Attuned to memory
and the redundancy
of the power system
it sets up.

Body seems slower,
            more withdrawn.

Each time you return
and find it slightly altered

when you
just want
to relax.

Pornography
but with the good parts
missing.

On a Saturday night
you should always
buy yourself something.

In the past
it would have been
a drink

but now
the old songs
sound terrible.

Clothes are
either too light
or too dark.

When the Moon Is Full

It's not unusual
for the face
to fill with fluid
or the hair
carelessly pinned
to grow wet.
When the moon is full
we often dream
that the dead
are back among us
and dying again.

In a Monotonous Dream

The language
created the landscape

and there was only
one word

which meant
at various times

depending on
the inflection

motherdeath
cabbagefangs

ominous headwaiter
sinister whirring

bad joke
rude uncle

song that is stuck
half-open window

lecturing priest and
bride that was never a virgin.

Thanksgiving Poem

Rose, you are American
as a three-cornered hat.
A worthy envoy
of our idealism,
go then and say
that we are grateful
to have such luck.
For the higher self
life is one good thing
to eat after another.
And people smile
at the superior one
for no reason at all
other than to confirm
that they believe
in his existence
which is of course
the cause of their dismay.

Aperture

The noose
rests lightly
on the lamp

Restraining
No   engaging it
to memorize

these details
that charisma
drawn from the well

of a broken circle

Puritans

There are no small ones.
All big-boned

men and women
without a hint of child's play.

They creak
as they walk

like doors left open
to bang in the wind.

One imagines from their gait
that years from now

they will make adroit bowlers.
Meanwhile, they whisper

careful not to sound rhythmic.
Dovegray, lavender and eggshell

are the only colors
and even these must be bleached, muted,

in order for their profiles
to emerge on cold cash

as if doodled there
with invisible ink.

If not optimistic,
they are eternally democratic

and can be handled
without contamination.

That word
has no meaning for them.

Touch them
as much as you like,

wherever you please.
They have never felt

the desire to reciprocate
and for that they are grateful.

Being Sick Together

In the postmodern world
the sequel is always superior

to the original
and it is even possible

for someone like Tony Perkins
to meet a nice girl in *Psycho III*

a suicidal former nun
who is also tormented

by sexual fantasies
so that he can teach her something

old-fashioned as dancing
the fox trot

and she can offer him
a drink in her room.

At the Bates Motel
water drawn from the same tap

where famous shower scene began
now seems pleasantly refreshing.

Surface Tension

1.
that feeling
of resignation
that comes
          before change

2.
someone calls
and says
she has seen a body
flying through the air

maybe now
isn't a good time
to talk

3.
fuck shapes

4.
replace the narrative
with another
form of narrative

5.
aping
the lush life

6.
the Hansel and Gretel
basement

the endless supply
of cookies

7.
the rarely seen
pistachio green

8.
privacy

9.
as another form of intimacy

10.
they call that
        a sucker punch

11.
when a woman
walks toward you

the way she did

something happens

12.
it's like mailing a letter

13.
you think of things
as coordinates

14.
you replace sleep
with pointing

The Myth of Self

There is the mask of a dead infant
whose head is small as a salt shaker
as well as the mask of Charlie Chan
the mask of long absences
and of course various satyrs
with furry cheekbones and webbed eyes.
There is also the mask of looking goofy
at your own party, designed to make others
think you are intoxicated while you
soberly judge them behind bloodshot slits.
There are masks, too, for men who wish,
if only for an hour, to become fat women
and scream at everyone, "Empty the ashtrays!"
And finally, there are simply ugly things
with green flesh and gold warts
designed to make people appreciate
the real you, the one who has no reflection.

Voodoo Doll

For you
everything is
calamity.
With your glazed
toad's eye,
delicate breath
in a jar
and wrists
of thread,
you do your magic
drudgery, sewing
grass to sky
root to flower
grudgingly.
And yet,
you are yourself
just thrown together
with wax and incantation.
At times almost
not there at all
but still tied
to the world
and restless.

And God Created Woman

To walk
with bare feet

joined
to color
candor

two simple
things

conveniently
fitting

or finding time
for expression

the go between
at the base
of a triangle

in a common
garden

a dowry
of clay

an instrument
for copying
coping

in the shape
of a nipple

To Amelia Earhart
Whose Birthday I Share

The day we were born
was mild as a ghost's breakfast

and after the Romantic Age
had finally finished its coffee

the butcher sliced our conversation.
It was to be my first solo

so I was nervous about being
out of place in the sky

though I needn't have been.
Flight came easily to me

as it did to you.
A mixed blessing

that makes walking
seem fantastically slow.

Seasons change
with the traffic light.

A dead woman
overtakes me on the street.

Reversal

Wing
pushes
through water's
         socket

a spray
of fingerprints
from which
we pluck
a musical note

Frozen
it hangs
cornice-like
above the opalescent
         slate

Sheer membrane
that separates
the image
from its opposite

The Foreign Legion

It's pleasant
to wake
to a camel's nuzzling
even on the run.
Glorious,
not to give a hoot
about anything
and say so
but best of all
is the exotic way
everything normal
begins looking
in order to
win you back.
How the moment
in need
of being rescued
turns its helpless eye
toward you
as you
draw your sword,
reckless and lonesome.

After a Promising Youth

Once on vacation
he threw the pyramids
a curveball
and ever since
it's been hopeless.
Now a dishwasher
he works
in a Tarot Card
above the city.
Cooped up all day
in the fairy-tale sky,
evenings he sings dirges.
Weekends he likes to be
tied up and whipped.

They Looked Like Brother and Sister

He wore striped breeches
and a pumpkin vest.

Sat at the piano with his knees wide apart
and played vigorously

like a nice kid
who'd grow up to be a jerk.

She never shut her mouth.
Margaret was always

practicing a son,
with a pile of sheet music the size of *War and Peace*

on her lap.
First, she'd recite all the words aloud

before turning that milky soprano loose
in a room full of cherubs and artificial flowers.

Perfect Little Philistines
is what someone said after a recital

and with well-shined shoes.
One day that candelabra

will be all that remains
of his Liberace youth

but her,
I worry about.

So innocent,
Walt Disney gives her palpitations.

So impractical,
she can't decide which season is loveliest.

At the Dante Alighieri Photo Booth

Breath
develops film

but who would not
appear poetic

when placed before
good background's
old velvet

or under
heavy
planet's influence

Breakfast with Jerome

Light shivering on its tightrope

Bizet in the background

Banana bread and a pear

Swinging its lantern of white noise

The chef's hat perches on the fence

The coachman is driving the city to the city

Magically the page refills itself

Common Knowledge

In Egypt
everything was fragrance
all the time.

A slight
molecular
                wind

and the
jackal-headed god
would sniff
you out.

*

Without
the 100 words
for snow

scent is quick

like hormones
in bumper cars.

After six days
the child
knows its mother
by smell

lilacmilk
hairsprayknives.

Things to Do in the Bible

Get drunk.
Walk on water.
Collect foreskins.
Pluck out an eye.

Build an ark.
Interpret dreams.
Kill your brother.
Don't look back.

Join a tribe.
Listen to clouds.
Live in a tent.
Quit your job.

Take to the hills.
Report to the king.
Raise the dead.
Seek the spirit.

Reap what you sow.
Count your blessings.
Gnash your teeth.
Fish for men.

Grow a beard.
Wear a cowl.
Ride a donkey.
Carry a torch.

Sit by a well.
Live to a ripe, old age.
Remain a virgin
and speak in tongues.

These are the words of the Lord.

Postcard

We untie the river.
We read the river.
There is no river
but we follow it anyway
and sometimes when skimming
a light from its history
we think, how pleasant
it is to say "we"

we think these things
while walking by the river.

You Go to My Head

The outcome was
unexpected
           a light silly note
           on the table
after rowing like a galley slave
to open the bronze door
           and still in my
"journey to the center of the earth"
           rags,
I come home to find
such music as I've never heard pour
from the dolphin-headed faucets.
It's just that I had pictured
something more dramatic
           than a cocktail.
Who thinks of such things
           in a gloomy old cave?
"But my dear," you said
winding a towel around your head,
"it doesn't take a genie
to see you're destined
           for fun,
and awful as it sounds
you must learn to make the best of it."

Tabloid for Topcat

Riveted and
re-visiting

behind the scene
        curtain calls
the nuts and bolts
of it

       Spurs
old records
round a dusty bin

They sound good again
here   with you

where Maria Callas
serves the coffee

in a stellar way
that counts

Escape from Women's Prison

1.

We had almost forgotten what men were,
the part they played in our downfall.
On our breaks in the yard
where the air smelled of shampoo
we thought of ourselves as almost good
and it was only occasionally
that one or the other
heard a voice from outside call.
"There was plenty of dope in Florida," Annie'd say,
"and we smoked it all in convertible cars and Holiday Inns."
Then she'd stop, like she was trying to picture something
and each time she told it, the story got shorter.
It was the same for everybody.
In the heat of the workroom,
we'd hallucinate zippers
but when their clothes fell away,
there was only the long rows of washboards.
"If ever there were men on this planet," Iris mumbled,
"they existed a long time ago."

2.

Another time the warden
sent us out to pick strawberries, two by two.
"Are you thinking about men?"
We were on our backs in this field.
The plants were real short
so we had to lay down if we wanted any shade.
I was thinking about church.
"Jesus was a man," I said.
"Yeah, but not the one I'm thinking of. This one
had eyes that were always chatting."
"Do you think they watch? Sometimes I get the feeling
that the whole prison is surrounded by men.
Sometimes I get the feeling all we'd have to do is ask
and they'd take us anyplace we wanted to go."

54

Generic

Who is
that statue
a state of?

Why it could
be anyone.

Shifting thru
        anathema's
litter

generic
as a puff
of flag

or the bullet-headed
beam
        of an apple.

Aleister Crowley Slept Here

There is something banal about evil
but the reverse is also true
and what is mundane quickly becomes sinister.
Like the building on the corner
where his ghost tampers with a geranium.
So ordinary yet gloomy,
one senses he was bored
and this can be verified
in his autobiography, wherein he states,
"I confess to dislike Chicago . . .
It gives the impression of being a pure machine."
Of his apartment, there is not much to see.
A Weber grill, pale yellow and never used
that the new tenants installed on the balcony.
If I meet them, I will ask
if they have nightmares often
although it is not likely.
He was older when he resided here.
Pretty much the retired Prospero
who'd broken his wand in favor of literature.
A mistake, in this city, as he found out
when calling on the editor of Poetry magazine.
A poetess, of whom he writes,
"I am still not sure if she knew my name
and my work, but she showed no interest whatsoever!"
As you see, things haven't changed.
I live down the street
and often he haunts the neighborhood
searching, as I am, for this or that line.
And after storms I always think
those knots of wet string
you find coiled on the sidewalk
must surely have belonged to him.

Readers Answer Romance

Air
more solid
than flesh
a slate

of intersected
      speaking

not just the
cool cloth
of the head

              but also
              earth

              and the low
              flame

              of the sun
              and the slow
              pulse

              of the stone

Frida Kahlo

like mint
growing

in a patch
of weeds

cool
on the edge

inventing yourself
as you went along

inventing
brilliant colors

to dress
and address

the ghost
in you

How Sue Feels about the West

My dreams
are like the Midwest
mostly flat

but every now and then
a big city
comes out of nowhere.

They just go and go
until they reach the ocean,
then they stop

but you say
you understand the West
because you're more bossy,

when your kids wake up early
you don't think, "Charming"
you think, "Those brats"

while I am always
telling my thoughts
like a novel.

I can't help it.
Those were my favorite parts
where the guy would say,

"We were both nude
in the water.
My first thought was —"

or else,
"I wrestled the pajama top
off her and thought —"

"Thoughts, thoughts,"
you say with a shrug,
"I haven't time.

This morning my husband
fried the skin off his hand
in the toaster,

but one thing
I do understand
is the West.

I know it very well
and why things work
the way they do there.

That's not the problem,
the problem is
no one understands

how I feel
about the West
about living here, I mean."

A Bouquet of Objects

Lovely to be
like a racehorse surrounded by flowers

but it is also lovely
to be surrounded by air and own pendants

and bracelets of soot.
Here is a factory made fresh by broken windows

and there is my muse
returning home with a pail of milk.

He brings me
down to earth where all poetry begins

with such beautiful hands
that I am forever doing nothing but thinking

of objects
and asking him to hold them.

To La Rochefoucauld

such is
the power of words
to move things

when taken
from its shelf
the horse gallops
into the shadows
under the table

Pale Yellow

Of course I
want your approval
        desperately

as I want
a second cup
        of coffee.

The morning slips
out of its tee shirt.
        A chill,

pale yellow
big bunch of lilies
        billowing

holds my attention
in mid, not flight,
        so much as upward clamor.

Reflections of a vaguely
southwestern "el Navajo
        fire-escape" pattern

paint the window
across the street.
        I want to lick them off.

For David Hockney

Cock sweet.
Wind studied.
Housework
complete.
Pool lacquered
like a Turkish
cigarette case.
Nice light.
Book in bed.
The hours strike
sotto voce.

To Avoid Confusion

She holds them
in separate hands:

this is coherence

this is continuity

Wet Dreams

The streets
are flooded

she says
sliding down
a waterfall

so I leave
my cigarettes
at the bottom
of the stairs.

You know
how he is.
Everyone is
already changed.

The nudity
gets our attention
then lets it
wander.

Brick paints
bridge and river
medieval brown.

It was the diary
of a sloppy life
so they gave it up.

In his highchair
the lifeguard reads
the liquid paper.

With his birds-
eye-foot he rocks
the pool.

Summary

My dreams
                  unassembled
resemblance to a
ride in the country
                  you've seen
it all
but especially think
you've seen
that tree before
                  no matter
it's the words
that are important
                  but there aren't any

Last Night of the Year

Listen with your eyes
With all the senses
Take things home
to the present tense

Black coffee
Green grapes
              Paper
white narcissus

Lines that intersect
create their own drama
and the distance
between is actually
a form of participation

You didn't know that
not really
              until now
or you wouldn't
have insisted
on adding so much

To and Fro

for Jerome

I am
the four walls'
maiden name

and this is
the freeze-dried groom
who goes
with anything

that point
where white
swirls into black

on television
where someone is
always getting married
to boost
the ratings
until everyone
is married

Then they begin
renewing their vows